E.E. Wilkins

The Purposeful®
Husband

Become the Husband God Has Called You to Be
(And the Husband Your Wife Needs You to Be)

HAWTHORNE GRAYSON PUBLISHERS LLC

Katy, Texas 77491

HawthorneGrayson Publishers
P.O. Box 6912 Katy, TX. 77491

ISBN: 979-8-9890788-0-6 (print)
ISBN: 979-8-9890788-1-3 (eBook)

Ordering Information:

Special discounts are available on quantity purchases by churches, corporations, associations, and others. For details visit: eewilkins.com or email eew@eewilkins.com or call 281-809-3885.

Library of Congress Control Number: 2025913043

Edited by Joseph Adams Sr.
Cover photo by Pearl via Lightstock.com
Book cover designed by Kamrul Hasan
Interior Formatting by Anointing Productions
The Purposeful is a registered trademark of E.E. Wilkins

1st Edition / 2025

*This book is dedicated to the person who befriended me,
and chose to mentor me in becoming a Godly Husband.
This book is dedicated to Graddie Peoples.*

Contents Page

pur·pose·ful

ˈpərpəsfəl/

adjective

adjective: **purposeful**

1. having or showing determination or resolve.
"the purposeful stride of a great lawyer"

"the purposeful stride of a great lawyer"

synonyms: determined, resolute, steadfast, single-minded;
More enthusiastic, motivated, committed,
dedicated, persistent, dogged, tenacious,
unfaltering, unshakable "she'll need a more
purposeful attitude if she wants to succeed in
college"

antonyms: aimless

o having a useful purpose.

"purposeful activities"

o intentional.

"if his sudden death was not accidental, it must have been purposeful"

Acknowledgments

I could not have written one word without the eternal grace of God, my Lord, and Savior. This book had to be written by someone, and I am humbled God chose me to birth it into fruition.

I want to thank my parents Augustine and Gloria (Hawthorne) Wilkins for encouraging me to pursue my dreams. To my Crossover Bible Fellowship family, thank you for providing the Men's Ministry programs to equip men to become the husbands God had called us to be. I am thankful for our leadership team consisting of lead Pastor Blake E. Wilson, Elders Reggie Holiday, Royce F. Robinson, Harold Washington, and Artis Wilson, for their continuous guidance and wisdom. I also want to thank Joseph Adams, Jeffrey Bailey, Daniel Beard, J. Michael Frasier, Graddie Peoples and Craig Wright for investing in me and showing me what a Purposeful Husband looks like.

I want to acknowledge my godfather Willie Skillern for always being present in my life and modeling a Godly Husband for me. I want to thank my mentors Gilbert Bigham Sr., Elmo Flanagan, David Fleming, the late Hubert Hawthorne, and Henry Jones Sr., who told me the truth rather than what I wanted to hear. I want to thank my pastors, the late Claude A. Berry of New Mount Carmel Missionary Baptist Church in Houston, Texas and Pastor Walter Kyle Berry Sr. of McGhee Chapel Missionary Baptist Church in Houston, Texas and the late Pastor J. E. Wilkins Sr. of Mount Olive Baptist Church in Simonton, Texas. Although there are many more, these men all helped to shape and mold my foundation in God's word. Finally, I want to thank the four people who chose to be transparent and make The Purposeful Husband Manuscript what it is. By sharing their personal stories, perspectives and how God is working on them, it gave me hope. In turn, I pray this book will bless others like it has blessed me. To Ronald Ben, Richard Jackson, Alexander Williams, and Carlos Willis, I could not have completed the book without your testimonies, encouragement, and prayers. I am eternally grateful to you and your wives. Thank you for standing up and deciding to take this journey with me.

E.E. Wilkins

Purpose

The purpose of this book is to encourage married men to become better husbands. To become better husbands, we must face the harsh reality that we cannot do it alone, first, we need to be filled with the Holy Spirit, then be willing to be challenged by other godly men so that we can properly lead our families. In general husbands may have similar backgrounds and upbringings and are accomplished business leaders in their respective professions, however few husbands are leading based on the way God calls husbands to lead. Oftentimes, this is due to a lack of actually seeing a Godly Husband being modeled in our homes as we are growing up. We cannot lead by example if there was no example. This book will address strategic ways we can become better husbands by making consistent changes and corrections to our mindsets and actions when it pertains to taking on God-given responsibilities.

Introduction

Imagine showing up to work and your supervisor gives you keys to a helicopter and tells you, "Go fly across town." Without the proper training and practice hours, you wouldn't stand a chance of making it across town. Similarly, after getting married you immediately take on the responsibility of being spiritually responsible for your bride and any children in your new possibly blended family. Without proper training, you are guaranteeing yourself future pain and suffering due to a lack of education; therefore if you love your family, it is your responsibility as a husband to get the tools and skills necessary to lead our families.

Consider this: Jesus spent thirty-three years on earth as fully God, fully man and demonstrated leadership in every situation. He experienced anger, disappointment, criticism and other feelings we go through, but he successfully endured without failure. As men, we should not be focused on re-inventing the wheel. The blueprint for being a Godly husband has clearly been outlined for us in the bible. God loves us so much, he has left a written manual for us to model ourselves after. We no longer need to guess, speculate, wonder, or figure out how to be the biblical husbands God has called us to be. We simply need to follow his biblical playbook. In sports, successful teams are the ones that study, prepare, train, and mentally focus on weekly game plans. Similarly, as godly husbands, we have to create a daily habit of studying God's word, preparing our hearts, and training our minds to mentally lock in on God's plan for our marriage.

CHAPTER ONE

Identifying the Problem

"When I have learned to love God Better than my earthly dearest, I shall love my earthly dearest better than I do now."
-C. S Lewis

CHAPTER 1

Identifying the Problem

Most married men want to be better husbands and leaders for their wives and family. The problem is we simply do not know how. It is virtually impossible to become a Purposeful Husband without being exposed to one. In most urban areas, especially those from single-parent households, young men are not taught God's guidelines for leading a family. This is not to say mothers are not trying. Unfortunately, we have women who do their best to raise young men based on God's instructions. It is simply a matter-of-fact women cannot teach a boy how to be a man. God has not given her the ability to be the husband leading their families, that assignment is solely directed at the husband. This is the result of persistent problems of absentee fathers in today's society. Our fathers who were not present and involved

"Marriage is patterned after Christ's covenant relationship to His redeemed people, the church.

in our lives failed to show us what a godly husband and leader looks like. Consequently, we are following suit by providing the same lack of presence to our sons and daughters. In order to turn the corner on this epidemic, we first must begin by changing how we view God and his design for husbands and fathers so that we are better equipped to interact with our kids. Our children's lives and futures are at risk when we fail to live up to our fatherly positions and responsibilities.

Another problem we face is **selfishness**. No one wants to admit they are selfish, but we are, and we want what we want. We do not want God's will for our lives; we want our desires and thoughts for our lives. Add in **stubbornness** and being **prideful** and you have the perfect ingredients for a failed marriage. **Basically, when you get married you have two selfish people coming together to have "their own way."** The problem is when you say "I DO" it is no longer about you. God never said marriage is about your happiness. Marriage is designed for God's glory. In his article titled, *The True Purpose of Marriage*, John Piper said, "Marriage is patterned after Christ's covenant relationship to His redeemed people, the church. And therefore, the highest meaning and the most ultimate purpose of marriage is to put the covenant relationship of Christ and His church on display."

We were not put on this earth to run around like animals and procreate with every woman we see. Likewise, women need to stop opening their legs and allowing everyone to enter their wombs and violate their bodies physically, spiritually, and mentally. Realize that after you have sex with someone, you are now emotionally connected to that person, which not only causes mental anxiety and problems between the two of you but could result in creating another generation of messed up and confused young men and women. Additionally, some men want to remain little boys well into their thirties, living with their parents, playing video games, and never taking responsibility for their lives. These individuals relish the idea of going to a part-time job, then heading to the gym to exercise. Most evenings are spent dating multiple women and running the streets with friends. Some husbands have even carried this behavior into their marriages. They rarely have time for their families because they prefer to spend time with friends. By the time the bar/club closes or their friends send them home, it is time to go to bed and start another day. This cycle continues all week until one day you wake up and your kids are grown, and your wife has all but checked out of the marriage. Surely, we know this is not what God intended for our marriages. Yet we do not consult God when we are indulging in sin. We do not recognize this is a problem until we come home to an empty house. God designed us to be spiritual leaders and protectors of our families. The problem is we are rejecting God's plan for our lives and focusing on what the flesh desires. There is no other place to point the finger at other than ourselves. Some of us did not drop the ball. We simply decided not to even pick it up in the first place. We must ask ourselves are we following God's design for our lives or are we leaning on our own understanding and going through the motions. The truth is, it does not matter how many accolades we receive at work; if you are not spiritually leading your family at home, God is not pleased with you. You will be held accountable for your actions. I urge you to confess it, repent, and ask God for forgiveness. God does not make mistakes if you purchased this book, or it was purchased for you, then you are supposed to have it in your hands reading it. Be obedient and read each chapter along with the Purposeful Husband Points of Reflection's and corresponding scriptures. Have your bible or device next to you to readily access the scriptures. Use the Notes and Reflection areas to document and record your thoughts and takeaways from each chapter. Then apply those points and your notes in your daily life and watch God move in your marriage.

Points of Reflection

1. A Purposeful Husband determines if he was exposed to Godly leadership growing up and imitates their faith. Hebrews 13:7

2. He admits when he is selfish, stubborn, and prideful. Philippians 2: 3-4, Proverbs 16:18

3. He confesses and repents. 1 John 1:19

Notes and Reflection

_____

_____

_____

_____

_____

_____

_____

_____

_____

_____

_____

_____

_____

_____

_____

_____

_____

_____

_____

_____

_____

_____

_____

_____

_____

_____

CHAPTER TWO

Am I Ready to Lead?

(How Ready Is Ready?)

"Relationship is fostered through conflict."
-Dr. Crawford Loritts

CHAPTER 2

Am I Ready to Lead?

(How Ready Is Ready?)

I remember about a year into my marriage, all of a sudden, I had an epiphany. After months of frustrating my wife with the daily fact that I did not have a clue about being a husband, I decided I needed to take action. I contacted my four-year-old son's godfather who was married with children. We agreed to meet at a pool hall and talk over a game of billiards. I remember looking him dead in the eyes and saying hey, I am terrified about being a husband and father. His response caught me off guard. He said, "Are you spiritually prepared to lead your family?" I thought about it for a moment and responded, "No, I know I'm not spiritually prepared to be neither one of

> *We spend more time helping our future wife plan out the wedding but fail to plan out the marriage.*

those." Without judgment or contempt, he told me to go get the tools I needed to lead my family.

In life, as men we know to do certain things in order. Before we decide to change the oil on our cars or replace the brake pads on our vehicles, we prepare for the job by grabbing the specific tools we need to complete the job. Whether it is a socket set, wrenches, or pliers, we know we cannot break loose one bolt without the proper tools. However, when it comes to our wives and children, we often show up empty-handed trying to make do with a rusty pair of pliers, instead of obtaining the specific tools (information) we really need for the job. If we were to give ourselves a grade on how we prepare as husbands most of us would score a D minus or F daily.

The scripture says in Deuteronomy 24:5 (NASB), "When a man takes a new wife, he shall not go out with the army nor be charged with any duty; he shall be free at home one year and shall give happiness to his wife whom he has taken." What the bible is saying that when you get married you need to take one full year learning your wife. Spend time getting to know her and learning how to make her happy. We spend more time helping our future wife plan out the wedding but fail to plan out the marriage. Think back to the time before you got married. You spent hours upon hours talking on the phone, courting her, and taking her out on dates. You were committed to getting to know her hopes, dreams, wishes, and desires. You went above and beyond trying to make all of them come true. Now that you are married, you will not even plan out a dinner date or evening out. After showing her how dedicated you were to her being happy, now you are only concerned with fulfilling your own sexual desires before bedtime. Old folks say, "What you did to get her, you better continue to do to keep her." Falling into complacency can only lead to marital frustration and bitterness from your mate. You do not want your spouse going to bed reminding you of how you used to treat her. This behavior will ultimately lead to long nights of loneliness.

Points of Reflection

1. Get spiritually prepared to lead your family. Matthew 6:33, Romans 12:1-2, Timothy 3:4-5

2. Pray and ask God for wisdom and guidance. Galatians 5:16-26, James 1:5-8

3. Learn your wife, and study her and how to make her happy. 1 Peter 3:7, Ephesians 5:25-33, Colossians 3:12-14

4. Find two brothers spiritually mature to mentor you and hold you accountable in your marriage. Proverbs 13:20,15:22, 27:17

5. Obtain the proper tools for the job before you start. Proverbs 24:27, 2 Timothy 3:17

Notes and Reflection

CHAPTER THREE

Ready, Set-Go

"God uses adversity & storms to show you who he is."
- BLAKE WILSON

CHAPTER 3

Ready, Set-Go

Now that we have all the pleasantries out of the way, let us dive into the word. First, now that you have made the conscious decision to become a Purposeful Husband you can expect all Hell to come your way. You can expect problems at home; your wife and kids will begin acting a fool. Problems with your parents, in-laws, and issues at work.

You may even experience a lack of peace while you are trying to sleep. The bible says in Ephesians 6:12 (NIV), "For our struggle is not against flesh and blood, but against the rulers, against the authorities, against the powers of this dark world and against the spiritual forces of evil in the heavenly realms." Understand me when I tell you the devil will be coming at you on all angles to get you off track and destroy your focus. It is imperative you put on the whole armor of God right now. According to Ephesians 6:10-17, you need the full armor of God to be strong in the Lord and use his strength so you can stand firm against the many schemes of the devil. Verses 14-17 says, "Stand firm therefore, Having

Girded your LOINS WITH TRUTH, and HAVING PUT ON THE BREASTPLATE OF RIGHTEOUSNESS, and having shod YOUR FEET WITH THE PREPARATION OF THE GOSPEL OF PEACE; in addition to all, taking up the shield of faith with which you will be able to extinguish all the flaming arrows of the evil one. And take THE HELMET OF SALVATION, and the sword of the SPIRIT, which is the word of God." This is what we are called to do, so do not run from it, or stray away from it, embrace it as part of the process. Dr. Tony Evans says, "When you are in labor giving birth, it's painful excruciating times, pushing you to the point of passing out from exhaustion

> *"Change never arrives dressed up in fancy clothes and wearing three-piece suits.*

and just before you quit and give out, you give birth to a new creation. Oh, it's gon hurt. It's going to cost you unbearable grief, and downright misery. But ask any new mother after giving birth and she is holding her baby, was it worth it." This is true for husbands as well as when we decide to take our proper positions as spiritual leaders in our families. Dr. Evans continued by saying, "Change never arrives dressed up in fancy clothes and wearing three-piece suits. It is hard, intensive labor and requires you to get down on your knees in the mud and filth that has been plaguing your marriage for a while."

In January of 2016, one Saturday morning while going through the 33 Series, our pastor, Blake Wilson gave us a visual analogy of the Hand-off. He said, "Imagine being in the Super bowl game and you are the quarterback. You are facing the number one defense in the NFL, and you are under the center getting ready to hike the ball. All you need is one yard to score the winning touchdown and there are five seconds left in the game. You are in the I-formation with one running back behind you, your wife. And you snap the ball and say, "Here, honey, go get that one yard!" And you send her into that angry defensive line. What do you think the outcome will be, with everybody watching around the world on National TV?"

As men, when we do not step into our roles as husbands and fathers to our children, that is what we are doing! In fact, that is exactly what we are doing daily. Handing the ball to our wives and sending them into battle to get annihilated through our omission to walking in our calling as husbands. Some of the responsibilities we are handing off include:

Spiritual Leadership	**Prayer Life**
Family Vision	**Loving Attitude**
Finances	**Serving Spirit**
Willingness to Listen	**Forgiveness**

As difficult as it may be, as husbands we need to take inventory of ourselves and determine where we are in the process of being a Purposeful Husband. In the next chapter, we will look at steps you can take to improve your relationship with your spouse and how you lead your family.

Points for Reflection

1. A Purposeful Husband understands in marriage not stepping up equals stepping aside. 1 Timothy 3:4, Ephesians 5:25

2. He Knows husbands have to lead by example. Colossians 3:19,

3. He recognizes that passivity in marriage cripples his spouse. 1 Peter 3:7

4. He understands that God wants him to lead. 1 Corinthians 11:3

5. He knows being a strong example for his sons, shows his daughters what true manhood looks like because he is their visual bible in the home. Proverbs 20:7, 22:6

Notes and Reflection

_____

_____

_____

_____

_____

_____

_____

_____

_____

_____

_____

_____

_____

_____

_____

_____

_____

_____

_____

_____

_____

_____

_____

_____

_____

CHAPTER FOUR

The Corporation

(Developing Your Family Vision)

"A man without a map will be a man without a spine; he'll lack both conviction and courage. A man without a map will be a man without a heart; he'll lack both passion and compassion."
-DARRIN PATRICK

CHAPTER 4

The Corporation

(Developing Your Family Vision)

Corporations like Apple, ExxonMobil, Shell, and Halliburton do not become successful companies out of happenstance. For any company large or small to operate efficiently, certain things must be in place. There must be organizational wings consisting of marketing, research and development, and accounting departments in place to maximize productivity. Each department has its own specific chain of command to lead the department to a common goal. When you get married, you and your spouse become the corporation. It is imperative that you have a strategic plan in place as to how you will structure your company. There has to be a CEO, COO, and CFO to maximize your company's potential. The best CEO to have running

> *The best CEO to have running your corporation is God.*

your corporation is God. There simply is no one more qualified you can have in that position. Likewise, you will serve as your Chief Operations Officer (COO) who oversees daily operations as directed by your CEO; and you will be responsible for ensuring the corporation's guidelines are implemented and adhered to. Your wife would follow suit by serving as the Chief Financial Officer (CFO), overseeing the books, and working closely with the COO to maintain unity within the corporation. Now, that is not to say the COO cannot be the CFO; however, God made your spouse to be a helpmate and work with you. We sometimes as men, forget to include our wives in decision-making and often pay the price for not utilizing her strengths.

Most businesses create and have readily available a company operation manual or procedures manual. It is critical that every business draw up operating practices and guidelines so that their corporation stays on course. Luckily, for us, God took the time to provide us with his love letters to the world that contains all the information we need. I remember hearing the Brenham brothers speak at the Dr. Tony Evans No More Excuses Conference in 2015. They were former baseball players who started their own real estate business. When asked how they having no experience become one of the top real estate firms in New Jersey. They answered by saying they structured their business based on God's biblical principles. This ultimately led to their success with their staff and employees understanding their company's expectations.

As you design and develop your family business manual be sure to implement God's plan into it. Schedule weekly meetings to create an itinerary of what topics you plan to cover and be sure to set a firm start and stop time to ensure punctuality. Identify strengths and weaknesses and take steps to correct and insulate your marriage from attacks and outside influences.

Another vital component to include in your Family Operations Manual is the establishment of boundaries, especially when it comes to dealing with in-laws, extended family, and close friends. While loved ones may have good intentions, their involvement can sometimes blur the lines and bring unnecessary strain into your marriage. As a corporation, it's essential that you and your spouse agree on what is acceptable and what is not when it comes to external influences. Clear boundaries allow your marriage to flourish without the noise and expectations of outside voices. The decisions made within your home must remain between the two of you and your CEO(God). Once outsiders are allowed to cross those lines unchecked, confusion can creep in, disrupting the order God intended for your household.

In addition to boundaries, your family corporation should also have guidelines in place for how and when conflict is addressed. One effective strategy is agreeing on a set time frame for bringing up concerns or offenses. For example, you and your spouse may decide that each person has 24 to 48 hours to speak on something that is bothering them. Once that window has passed, the issue is no longer allowed to be resurrected. This principle, as highlighted by Elder Royce F. Robinson in his 2015 sermon "Managing Marital Conflict" at Crossover Bible Fellowship, is rooted in discipline and grace. Robinson stated, "Conflict is necessary for growth and improvement." By dealing with conflict in a timely, respectful, and structured manner, couples avoid festering wounds and instead use friction as fuel for greater unity. When you know how to fight fairly and with purpose, you eliminate the chaos and allow peace to have a permanent seat at your table.

Lastly, always remember that your Marriage Manual of Operations is a living document. Just like any successful company updates its policies to reflect growth and change, your family vision should remain flexible and open to revision. Seasons of life will shift, children may come, careers may change, financial goals may evolve, and your operations manual should reflect those shifts. Think of it not as a rigid rulebook, but as a guiding framework of your personalized blueprint for sustaining love, faith, and order in your home. It is your set of "rules of engagement" to navigate life's inevitable highs and lows with unity, clarity, and peace.

In this corporation called marriage, success is not found in perfection, but in preparation. With God at the head, a united mission between spouses, and a solid manual to guide your journey, your family business is destined to thrive.

As the Word reminds us in Habakkuk 2:2–3 (NIV) "Then the Lord replied: 'Write down the revelation and make it plain on tablets so that a herald may run with it. For the revelation awaits an appointed time; it speaks of the end and will not prove false. Though it linger, wait for it; it will certainly come and will not delay.'"

Write the vision. Make it plain. Then trust God to bless the work of your hands and the covenant of your marriage.

Points for Reflection

1. A Purposeful Husband establishes a family corporation. Proverbs 16:3

2. He develops a Business Practices Manual and Mission Statement. Habakkuk 2:2-3

3. He addresses Purpose, Goals, Finances, Home Affairs and Vacations. 1 Timothy 5:8, Ephesians 4:15-29

4. He identifies strengths and weaknesses in his marriage and takes necessary steps to fortify his marriage. 1 Peter 4:10, Ephesians 4:2-3, 1 Corinthians 16:14

Notes and Reflection

_____

_____

_____

_____

_____

_____

_____

_____

_____

_____

_____

_____

_____

_____

_____

_____

_____

_____

_____

_____

_____

_____

_____

_____

_____

CHAPTER FIVE

Finances

Financing Your Corporation

"You must gain control over your money or the lack of it will forever control you."
-Dave Ramsey

CHAPTER 5

Finances

Financing Your Corporation

When it comes to finances nothing can put more stress on a marriage than money. The minute you get married you are now operating as one flesh. That means your corporation has two principal partners and everybody must be involved in the day-to-day business operations. I can honestly say I struggled with finances due to how I was raised and what I observed in my household. My mother was the primary breadwinner in my family. She worked in the oil and gas industry and made a decent salary every year. My father had his own landscaping business, but it did not pay much. He would spend most of his time working on mansions taking care of their grounds

As Purposeful Husbands we have to know how to handle our finances and lead by example.

and flowerbeds. He enjoyed the perks of being at expensive houses and taking care of wealthy clients. However, the flip side of that was that there were years when I made more money than my dad working part-time at the grocery store after school. Mother organized the bills and made sure everything was paid and my father basically deposited what he wanted in the bank and would be gone all day, seven days a week from 7am until 11pm at night. His passive approach to handling finances and not taking ownership or responsibility for the household became my reality of what a husband looked like. Consequently, this led to me growing up functionally illiterate when it came to handling finances.

As Purposeful Husbands, we have to know how to handle our finances and lead by example. We should also teach our children the value of learning how to manage their finances. If this is an area where you are weaker than your spouse, own up to that and communicate that to her. God knew we were not smart enough to handle everything on our own. That is why Genesis 2:18 says, "Then the LORD God said, "It is not good for the man to be alone; I will make him a helper suitable for him." This clearly tells us that God put our wives on earth to help us. Whether it is handling finances, or the daily operations of the household or simply being a listening ear, utilize her gifts and talents.

We live in a society where everyone wants to live separate lives. Single and married couples oftentimes never commit to building and becoming one flesh, resulting in early problems in the marriage. Some of the problems that arise in marriage could be a result of baggage that has been carried around for years. Sometimes we do not even realize we are packing around suitcases full of issues from previous relationships, family issues, hurt feelings, etc. It does not seem to manifest itself until you get married and all of a sudden it unleashes on your newly wedded spouse. How many times have you seen an argument coming before it started and wondered how did I know this was going to happen? It is not rocket science, it is simple actually, it is because you have seen it before. People tend to repeat patterns every so often. It is like listening to the same song over and over by placing it on repeat. We grow up telling ourselves, "I will never be like my father. I will not raise my family like he did." And a few years later, we see ourselves have become exactly like our farther. In fact, some of us have figured out how to master his behavior much better than he could have done it. The bible tells us in Numbers 14:18 that the sins of the father visit the son. We unknowingly do what we have been taught to do by visual images we observed growing up. The first person we try to emulate, is our father. Often, the first person we admire is our father. Subconsciously, someone may have been programed to think, operate, function, and respond just like our father responded to our mothers. It could be called hereditary, but I prefer to call it learned behavior. The best thing about learned behavior is that we can recognize it and unlearn the same behavior. It does take a focused effort to acknowledge our issues and correct them. However, scripture says in Philippians 4:13, "I can do all things through Him who strengthens me."

Points for Reflection

1. A Purposeful Husband utilizes his wife's strengths as a helpmate. Ecclesiastes 4:9-12

2. He doesn't treat his wife badly because he is still holding on to past hurt. Ephesians 5:33

3. He trust God in all aspects of his life, especially his finances. Philippians 4:19, Psalms 23:1, Matthew 6:25-34

4. He understands being passive in marriage is failing to act, protect and lead his family. Genesis 3:1-7, Ephesians 4:27

Notes and Reflection

CHAPTER SIX

Healing the Wound

(Pulling Back the Scabs)

"I am convinced that if we as a society work diligently in every other area of life and neglect the family, it would be analogous to straightening deck chairs on the titanic."
-STEPHEN COVEY

CHAPTER 6

Healing the Wound

(Pulling Back the Scabs)

If you have ever scraped your knee or wounded yourself, you have experienced the long process of healing and recovery. During this process, it is not uncommon for you to feel uncomfortable itching and tightness at the site of the wound. The minute you bump that injured area on your body and accidentally peel back the scab, you exposed raw skin and must restart the healing process all over again. The smart thing to do at this point would be to immediately sterilize the injured site and dress the wound by placing non-stick gauze on it, then closely monitoring it for the next few days for signs of infection. Likewise, as husbands, we sometimes wound our wives and get wounded in our marriage. We sterilize the injured site by apologizing and dressing the wound with non-stick gauze by trying to build that loving relationship back up. Finally, we monitor it closely for signs of infection by treating our spouses nicely for a period of time until the next argument comes up. Then we resort back to past behaviors and bring up every hurtful thing we can think of to win the argument. We men at times are our own worst enemies. We fall victim to the flesh, forgetting it is our job to love our wives like God loved the church. We neglect the responsibility of washing our wives in the word, and loving her unconditionally, no matter what comes out of her mouth. We have to always stay girded up and ready to forgive instead of focusing on the fight plan. No longer can we allow the enemy's desire to destroy marriages overrule our common-sense approach to resolving conflicts immediately when they arise.

> *We men at times are our own worst enemies. We fall victim to the flesh, forgetting it is our job to love our wives like God loved the church.*

Just as sure as you could bump that wound while walking around the house, you will have disagreements in marriage. There is no such thing as a marriage without disagreements. A perfect marriage is an unrealistic reality that only exists on a make-believe planet in another universe. What does God say about resolving conflict? Ephesians 4:31-32 says, "Let all bitterness and wrath and anger and clamor and slander be put away from you, along with all malice. Be kind to one another, tenderhearted, forgiving one another, as God in Christ forgave you." God is telling us to rid ourselves of those thoughts and actions so that when conflicts arise, you do not have those negative thoughts or actions in your head to fall back on. What is in your heart will eventually come out of your mouth. Dwelling on negative thoughts and actions often lead to negative responses in critical situations. Philippians 4: 8-9 says, "Finally, brethren, whatever is true, whatever is honorable, whatever is right, whatever is pure, whatever is lovely, whatever is of good repute, if there is any excellence and if anything worthy of praise, dwell on these things. The things you have learned and received and heard and seen in me, practice these things and the God of peace will be with you."

Ronald Ben is an educator who lives in Houston, Texas with his wife of 17 years, Keela Ben. I asked Ron to share a few lessons he has learned during their marriage, and his response was insightful. Ron said, "When I began to peel back the layers, I found out I brought several bags into my marriage. I am selfish, prideful, and manipulative. God has shown me that about myself through my spouse and several experiences that we have had. God has used my wife to teach me how to love like him. So, though I struggle with selfishness, pride, and a host of other things he challenges me via the Holy Spirit to sacrifice with no strings attached, he challenges me to dwell with my wife according to understanding versus trying to get my own way in situations and decisions we have to make. And he is teaching me to listen to my wife versus just trying to talk over her and dominate the conversation because I think I have all the right answers from the bible. I have learned that my wife knows as much bible as me, she just likes to express her feelings, and I need to listen and pay attention to her cues when she wants biblical answers or if she simply wants a listener at that moment."

Ron is not alone in recognizing he brought some unintentional baggage into the relationship. A lot of us have been hurt and scared but do not even realize we are wounded when we get married. We put our best foot forward when we are dating and appear perfectly fine while courting our prospective mates. It is not until after the wedding and honeymoon stage is long gone that our wounds are visualized, as they are rubbed in the relationship. Some of us were hurt during childhood, scared growing up, and never recovered from past hurts that we carried into adulthood; men often suppress issues, and painful memories, thinking they are fine because we do not acknowledge those hurtful experiences.

What stuck in my mind when I listened to Ron talk about his marriage was the fact he did not start off by pointing fingers at his spouse. He acknowledged and pointed out the fact that he brought wounds into his marriage he did not know he had. The second thing I observed about Ron was his recognizing he did not originally know how to listen to his wife. One of the biggest frustrations' wives incur in a marriage is the fact we husbands hear what they are saying but rarely listen to them. We need to understand there is a major difference in hearing and listening. An example would be we often hear music while we are driving our cars. But how often do we take time to listen to the messages that are within the songs? We hear the beat, melody and keep driving. Now imagine listening to the same song while driving knowing the radio station is giving away $1000 if you hear a random word like "Dupree" while the song is playing. You would focus on every word of that song trying to hear the word. Suddenly, the melody and beat become less important when you are motivated to concentrate. This is the approach we need to learn to master when communicating with our wives. We should be focused on every detail of their conversation with us to the point where we do not miss a single syllable. By changing the way we interact with our spouses, we can change the atmosphere in the home and eliminate some of the stressors within the marriage.

Imagine what would happen if your wife went off on you and instead of you going off in return, you told her how much you loved her, appreciated her, and understood her frustration. Her initial response would probably be anger because she would not know how to respond to receiving love instead of the usual venom you spew at her. However, if you consistently showed a loving pattern of behavior in these situations, she would have no choice but to accept the fact you are not going to return fire with fire in an argument. James 1:19-20 clearly tells us how to treat each other. Verse 19-20 says, "This you know, my beloved brethren. But everyone must be quick to hear, slow to speak and slow to anger, for the anger of man does not achieve the righteousness of God." We know what we need to do and how to accomplish the task at hand. The problem is we simply do not want to put forth the effort it takes to change. God is calling for us to go above and beyond our comfort zones. We are meant to truly lead our families. In the next chapter, we will look at some consequences of not bridling our tongues while allowing hurtful words to flow out of our mouths. As well as identifying some methods to correct the tendency to respond out of anger with our wives.

Points for Reflection

1. A Purposeful Husband forgives often. Matthew 6:14-15, 18:21-22

2. He loves unconditionally. Ephesians 4:31-32, 1 John 4:18

3. He focuses on positive things. Philippians 4:8-9, Colossians 3:2

4. He learns to listen without focusing on his response. James 1:19-20, 22-25

Notes and Reflection

_____

_____

_____

_____

_____

_____

_____

_____

_____

_____

_____

_____

_____

_____

_____

_____

_____

_____

_____

_____

_____

_____

_____

_____

_____

Loose Lips: The Power of the Tongue

"The mark of a spiritual man or women is a listening heart, not a lecturing tongue."
-GARY L. THOMAS

CHAPTER 7

Loose Lips: The Power of the Tongue

There will be days when your wife will say the most hurtful, mean-spirited, cutthroat, below the belt things to you. She may even go so far as to talk about your momma. How do you respond to the insults and put-downs directed square in your gut? Do you give her a piece of your mind? Do you say something equally as hurtful, or do you reflect on God's word and his grace he has shown you throughout your life? I would say choose to reflect on God's word and his grace and extend the same grace and mercy to your wife. Well, I do not have to tell you it takes a strong man to swallow his pride and love his wife even when she is acting unlovable. Proverbs 18:21 tells us, "Death and life are in the power of the tongue, and those who love it will eat its fruit." Purposeful Husbands cannot fall into the flesh and respond out of anger when conflict arises. We are

The deadliest weapon a married couple can wield between them is the tongue.

reminded of our responsibilities to lead our wives by washing them in the word. There are some rough edges we will have to smooth out and use gentle correction when handling our wives. During this time, we must continue to pray and ask God to give us the wisdom and scriptures to handle those situations with added grace and mercy.

James 1:26 says, "If anyone thinks himself to be religious and yet does not bridle his tongue but deceives his own heart, this man's religion is worthless." It is critical that you have a scripture in your head you can lean on when things reach a boiling point, and you are about to explode. I dwell on James 1:19-20 and repeat it to myself during the day to remind myself of how I am supposed to conduct myself. Verse 19-20 says, "This you know, my beloved brethren. But everyone must be quick to hear, slow to speak and slow to anger; for the anger of man does not achieve the righteousness of God." The scripture reminds us not to respond to insults and to remain calm while the hurtful things are being said to us. This is easier said than done because the flesh naturally wants to retaliate and respond in a like manner.

The deadliest weapon a married couple can wield between them is the tongue. It is best not to open your mouth if you are angry. Rather than speak out of anger, walk away, pray, read your bible, and ask God to order your thoughts and steps. Once you speak out of anger and allow hurtful words to leave your mouth, you cannot take it back. No matter how many times you apologize, your spouse is going to remember exactly what you said out of anger. It may take years to repair the damage of what you let slip off your tongue during a fit of anger.

Is it possible that the reason we say hurtful things is that there are things that may have occurred in our past that we unknowingly brought into our marriage? In the next chapter, we will look at what happens when we unintentionally bring hurtful baggage into our marriage and how it affects our relationships.

Points for Reflection

1. A Purposeful Husband meditates on James 1:19-20. Psalm 1, 119, Joshua 1:8

2. He does not speak out of anger. Proverbs 29:11, Ephesians 4:26-32

3. He shows grace and mercy to his wife. 1 Peter 3:7 Ephesians 5:25

4. He does not allow his tongue to speak freely. James 1:26, Proverbs 15:18

Notes and Reflection

CHAPTER EIGHT

Broken Pieces

"Many marriages would be better if the husband and the wife clearly understood that they are on the same side."

-ZIG ZIGLAR

CHAPTER 8

Broken Pieces

When you get married, you start with a pretty vase made of pure crystal. This represents your relationship between you and your wife. Over time dust starts to accumulate on it, and it does not get cleaned as regularly as before. Through anger and misunderstandings in communication, one of you accidentally knocks it off the table, and it breaks into pieces. Do you sweep it up and put it in the trash (divorce)? Or do you gather up the broken pieces and put them back together? I would argue you gather up the broken pieces and put them back together. Imagine if God would have thrown us away when we messed up or operated outside of his will for our lives. We are constantly falling short of living godly lives. Thankfully, God grants us new mercies every day. Lamentations 3:22-23 says, "The Lord's loving

If you are looking and searching for the perfect spouse, stop because they do not exist.

kindnesses indeed never cease, For His compassions never fail. They are new every morning; Great is Your faithfulness." We are supposed to emulate this same behavior when it comes to how we treat our wives.

If you are looking and searching for the perfect spouse, stop because they do not exist. We are all flawed, no one is perfect. The bible says in Jeremiah 17:9, "The heart is more deceitful than all else and is desperately sick; who can understand it?" Although we may view our deeds and actions as great, the bible says in Isaiah 64:6, "For all of us have become like one who is unclean, and all our righteous deeds are like a filthy garment, and all of us wither like a leaf, and our iniquities, like the wind, take us away. The scripture is telling us that on our best day we are as filthy as a women's menstrual rag full of blood. We are so caught up in our sins we cannot recognize just how far we have drifted out of God's will at times.

Ron Ben said, "During my season of unfaithfulness about seven years ago is when I literally stopped living out my life based on faith. This was around the time when my son was born. I didn't want to live and didn't care about my addiction and didn't care how it was damaging my family. We didn't fuss and fight; we just didn't talk to one another; our sex life was strained on top of that, and I was the cause of it all." Ron stated, "The only way we came out of our situation was through prayer. Though I had been exercising faith on so many levels, one thing that I was driven to do during this season was pray. My prayers were not really elaborate; it was just help me Oh God, Help me Oh God. God came through by my wife suggesting we go to another church, and my friend suggested Crossover Bible Fellowship, and this church took us in. Even though our marriage was headed down the tubes, the *Marriage Series: Till Death Do Us Part*, revived our marriage. We both did not serve for several years, we just sat at the feet of Jesus and healed all of our wounds. We still have scars and are being restored by grace but we are better because of God's grace shown to us by our local body. God caused us to feel so uncomfortable with our situation that we continued to pray. He answered our cries to live out a beautiful marriage before him, that could have easily turned into a disaster or lifetime movie."

Forgiveness is the sole reason we are still breathing and not living in eternal damnation. God's grace and mercy had covered all our transgressions that we may be presented as perfect. Yet we continue to live and operate as if we do not know God. We have become a society within the church that gives up on marriage and files for divorce quicker than folks who are not saved. We live in a microwave society that wants everything in thirty seconds. No one wants to put in the work it takes to build strong healthy relationships. We, as men, should understand our roles in the house. We are the spiritual leaders and are designed to shoulder the responsibility of taking on that role in our homes. The purposeful Husband forgives often and encourages his spouse daily.

Points for Reflection

1. A Purposeful Husband love unapologetically. 1 John 4:7-21, 1 Peter 4:8

2. He grants his wife forgiveness and grace daily. Mark 11:25, Ephesians 4:32

3. He meditates on God's word daily. Joshua 1:8, Philippians 4:8, Psalms 119:97-99

4. He studies his wife and learns as much about her as possible. Deuteronomy 24:5

5. He accepts responsibility and recognizes he is designed to carry her burdens, fears, and struggles without judging her insecurities. 1 Peter 3:7

Notes and Reflection

CHAPTER NINE

Running Towards Adversity

"Faith makes all things possible....
Love makes all things easy."
-DWIGHT L. MOODY

CHAPTER 9

Running Towards Adversity

We often shy away from adversity, especially when it shows up in our lives. God uses adversity in our lives to grow us up in our faith. According to Dr. Charles Stanley's sermon titled, *A Discerning Spirit*, we have two choices when we experience adversity in our lives.

a. Walk away from God

b. Walk with a deeper relationship with God

He stated adversity builds courage. In the book of Joshua chapter 1 verse 9 reads, "Have not I commanded thee? Be strong and of a good courage, be not afraid neither be thou dismayed, for the Lord thy God is with thee whither soever thou goeth," Dr. Stanley explained that

> *We need to learn to get out of the way and allow God to be God.*

adversity causes bitterness and often causes divorce. You should go to your bible at times of adversity and focus on God's word rather than your situation. No problem is bigger than God. We need to learn to get out of the way and allow God to be God. When we face difficult times, we should ask ourselves, "What is God trying to teach us, show us, or how is He trying to grow and mature us in a specific area of our lives." Spiritual maturity comes from God granting us spiritual discernment. Richard Jackson is a Network Engineer in the medical field. He has been married to Catreece Jackson for 14 years. Richard shared with me some of the struggles he experienced in his marriage. "The worst thing that has happened to me in my marriage was when my wife made many selfish decisions that could have ended our marriage based on the word of God. If my heart were focused on the pain and not Jesus, I would have ended it. Jesus said in Matthew 19:8-9 that it was the hardness of hearts that people divorce. Jesus kept my heart focused on Him and serving my wife." Richard stated if he could do it all over again, he would listen more to his wife. "I would try focusing more on the time when the Lord spoke through Catreece in the areas where I was falling short. At the beginning of our marriage, I battled with arrogance to the point where my wife would tell me what she was lacking in our marriage, and I ignored her. I wouldn't take it to heart or take action to make corrections because I didn't see anything wrong." Richard said during this time while dealing with adversity in his marriage he realized where he was not in alignment with God's will for his marriage and took steps to correct it. "I understand that now because I can see God's grace and mercy in my marriage that it is important that I show the same grace and mercy toward my wife and kids. God has taken me through many trials to develop my mind, heart, and soul to be submitted to him. I still have a long way to go but I am 100 percent his.

Richard's testimony outlined what can occur when we lose sight of the big picture and can no longer hear from God. Because we all have a lot going on and live busy lives, it is often easy to stray away from God's plan for our lives. As husbands when we are out of alignment with God, our entire family becomes out of alignment with God. Elder Royce Robertson once said, "Our relationship with our spouse is a direct reflection of our relationship with God." He concluded that if you are having problems with your wife not listening to you and experiencing confusion in your marriage, it is likely because you are doing the exact same thing with God.

As Purposeful husbands, we must study God's word so we can build up our discerning spirit. This spirit will help us to recognize the enemy's attacks early on. In addition, we must ask God to grant us the wisdom to recognize what he is trying to teach us. We must surround ourselves with Godly counsel. Who are you listening to daily? What kind of advice are these individuals giving you? Are they giving you advice based on God's word or leaning on their own understanding to advise you? Be careful who you are listening to. Pastor Blake Wilson often tells us to be careful who you are getting a word from. "Everybody has a word they want to share with you. The question is, where are they getting this word from?" he said. Having a discerning spirit allows you to have a keen ear when someone is telling you non-biblical doctrine. There are a lot of folks who quote the bible incorrectly or out of context. You must have a biblical foundation to recognize when you are being told something that is not based on scripture.

Points for Reflection

1. A Purposeful Husband embraces adversity. 2 Corinthians 4:8-9, James 1:2-4, 1 Peter 4:12-13

2. He refuses to operate in the flesh and walks in faith. Joshua 1:9, Hebrews 11:1, Proverbs 3:5-6, Galatians 5:16

3. He Focuses on God and not his situation. Romans 8:28, 2 Corinthians 1:4

4. He surrounds himself with Godly counsel/ mentors. Proverbs 13:20, Psalm 1:1

Notes and Reflection

CHAPTER TEN

Thoughts of Separation

"The greatest enemy to love is selfishness —putting self first instead of the needs of others, especially your spouse."
-BILLY GRAHAM

CHAPTER 10

Thoughts of Separation

What do I do when my wife no longer wants to be married? You turn it over to God. Pray and ask God to move in your marriage, that his will be done. Not your will, not your wife's will but his will. Continue to read God's word and stay focused on him and not the current circumstances you find yourself in. No problem, status, circumstance, or situation is greater than God. The bible says in Isaiah 54:17, "No weapon that is formed against you shall prosper; And every tongue that accuses you in judgment you will condemn. This is the heritage of the servants of the Lord, and their vindication is from Me," declares the Lord.

> *Purposeful Husbands cannot allow our flesh to respond out of anger towards our wives.*

Purposeful Husbands cannot allow our flesh to respond out of anger towards our wives. The Bible has already told us in 1 Peter 3:7 that she is the weaker vessel. And because it takes two people to argue we must be man enough and Godly enough to love our wives past the hurtful things she is saying and doing to us. James 1:26 says, "If any man among you seem to be religious, and bridleth not his tongue, but deceiveth his own heart, this man's religion is vain." What was noticed about this verse was not what was said, but how it was said: "If any man among you..." This suggests that it is expected for a wife to struggle with her tongue because she is the weaker vessel. We will struggle as well but God has placed husbands as the spiritual leaders of our households. We have an obligation to wash our wives in the word and remove the rough edges from her. Some call it dying every day: others call it spiritual maturity, either way, we have been charged with the responsibility of loving our wives like God loved the church. The amount of self-sacrifice and work it takes to walk upright and lovingly handle our wives in a mature manner has to be manifested from God. Left up to our own knowledge and understanding, we would not be able to stand up against the continuous barrage of insults and negativity associated with demonic personalities.

Under no circumstances am I suggesting you stand in place and allow your spouse to curse you or physically touch you in an aggressive manner. You should walk away and distance yourself until things calm down. No one should allow themselves to be subjected to abuse. Leave, even if it is going to another room or taking a walk around the block. Acknowledge your wife is upset and tell her, "I understand you are upset right now. I am going to take a walk and let things calm down and pray asking God for guidance in this situation. Let's agree to come together and discuss this in a specific time frame." You do not want to leave without acknowledging her frustrations and just ignore the fact she is upset about something.

More importantly, fall back on the rules of engagement that you agreed upon as to how you will handle arguments and disagreements. As Elder Royce Robertson puts it, "You have to understand the devil is crafty. He will look for any opportunity, weakness, or crack in your foundation to slip into your marriage and destroy it." One example would be, well we have rules of engagement, but we don't follow them or haven't implemented them. That is all the room the enemy needs to creep into your marriage. Another example would be the couple who is not getting along so one spouse decides to withhold affection from the other. Whether it is intimacy, or simply conversation, not spending time, or not sleeping in the same bed, it is a recipe for disaster. It leaves the door cracked open just enough for the devil to slither in and wreak havoc as days' past, and it becomes easier and easier not to talk or communicate with your spouse. Recognize the fact that even if you are not communicating at home, you will be talking to someone throughout the day, whether it is a coworker, church member, friend, or new acquaintance you met in passing. Before you know it, talking turns into going to lunch, then a dinner, or hanging out. A relationship begins to take form, and the devil starts organizing your thoughts in your head. His goal is to make his thoughts your thoughts. Before you know it, you begin to rationalize your actions. We are just eating lunch, two coworkers sharing a meal. Two lunches later, you cannot sleep, thinking about how much fun you had at lunch with that coworker. That is when the devil decides it is time to turn it up a notch. You begin having thoughts about what your coworker will be wearing today for lunch. It could be that you are dwelling on how considerate your coworker is or how they noticed you got your haircut. And why is it your spouse did not notice your new haircut or hairstyle? Similarly, it could be a new cologne you bought just to wear to lunch with your coworker. How is it possible that your wife has not noticed you smell better these days? What started out as an innocent lunch has grown into a committed relationship outside of your marriage; how did we allow this to escalate to this point, one step at a time, just one sin after the other? We must recognize one little sin births another sin: which leads to another sin, which keeps growing. The bottom line is that what we dwell on becomes our reality. Which is why we need to stay focused on God and his grace and mercy in our lives. Focus on how God loved us even when we were not loveable, and how God was faithful when we were faithless. Imagine what would have happened if God had not kept us when we were dead in our sin. Pastor Wilson often reminds us how we really wanted to go further in sin than we were already going, but God's grace protected us and kept us, even when we really wanted to sin.

Points for Reflection

1. A Purposeful Husband dwells on the Lord at all times. Galatians 5:1, Psalm 143:8

2. He focuses on implementing the scripture in your marriage. Ecclesiastes 4:12, Ephesians 5:25-33

3. He recognizes his wife is the weaker vessel and God wants him to wash her in the word. 1 Peter 3:7, Ephesians 5:26

4. He does not allow a window of opportunity for the devil to enter his marriage. Ephesians 4:26-27

5. He knows in marriage, absence does not make the heart grow fonder; it allows the enemy an opportunity to rise up in your marriage. 1 Peter 5:8

Notes and Reflection

CHAPTER ELEVEN

Break-up 101

"In too many marriage conflicts, we work too hard at winning the argument and too little at winning the heart."
-MATT CHANDLER

CHAPTER 11

Break-up 101

The Purposeful Husband handles break-ups with grace. If you happen to experience a separation while married there are certain things you should know. The first thing you should know about breaking up is it really hurts. It is nothing more painful than having to leave your home or watching your spouse leave you. According to the Bible, married couples should only separate for a time of prayer with an agreed upon time to get back together. 1 Corinthians 7:5 says, "Stop depriving one another, except by agreement for a time, so that you may devote yourselves to prayer, and come together again so that Satan will not tempt you because of your lack of self-control."

When you got married you made a covenant with God.

Unfortunately, the society we live in makes it acceptable to seek divorce at the first sign of disagreements among couples. Every day couples are throwing in the towel under the pretense of irreconcilable differences, which simply is not biblically sound. God will hold you accountable for walking out on your marriage. When you got married you made a covenant with God. Sometimes pride causes couples to incorrectly choose separation instead of counseling to resolve conflicts in marriage. There is no such thing as a perfect marriage. Marriage takes prayer, work, and dedication to continue building the marriage.

The enemy thrives in conflict and loves to cause dissension among couples. The minute you get married you are at war to stay married. If you do not remove strongholds, interfering in-laws, financial pressures, and pride from your relationship, you will not stand a chance of surviving your first five years of marriage. Outside influences in the form of friends, in-laws' and relatives lineup to cause confusion in new marriages. Couples should declare early that they will submit to God's authority in their marriage and follow his word. Genesis 2:24, instructs husbands cleave to your wives. However, we tend to do the exact opposite when it comes to obeying God's word. Instead of putting our wives first, we allow them to play runner-up to parents, friends, and our occupations; then we wonder why we are experiencing so much hell in our marriages.

Points for Reflection

1. A Purposeful Husband understands that just because she gives up on their marriage does not mean he has to do the same. Mark 10:9

2. He recognizes he is his wife's covering. Matthew 19:6

3. He remembers what 1 Corinthians 7:5 says about separation.

Notes and Reflection

CHAPTER TWELVE

Forgiveness on Steroids

"Forgiveness is a vertical commitment that is followed by a horizontal transaction."
-David Paul Tripp

CHAPTER 12

Forgiveness on Steroids

As a husband, understand that your wife will and is going to do things to hurt you, crush you, and demolish your heart. However, God requires you to love her anyway. The old folks would say anyhow, which means No Matter What. You just keep on doing what God has called you to do. As a Purposeful Husband, God is allowing you to experience the pain and suffering of this life to prune and mold you into the Husband Jesus was to the church. His love and grace were everlasting. According to John 14:27, we are given a peace that is not of this world but due to God's grace and mercy. Some may not be able to understand it. It allows us to forgive and handle situations others would not be able to comprehend, especially after being hurt and annihilated physically and mentally.

> *The Purposeful Husband does not allow anger to drive his emotions.*

Carlos Willis lives in Houston, TX and owns Kerygman Cuts Barbershop. He has been married to Sementa Willis for 16 years. Carlos experienced a lot of abusive relationships growing up with his mother in Jonesboro, Louisiana. Stemming from his mother's abusive boyfriends beating on him to improper behavior from his mom's female friends, Carlos began to struggle with anger and trust issues. Carlos said, "I wasn't saved at the beginning of my marriage so as a dead person in sin, I couldn't respond any differently. Basically, I was a puppet for the devil, and I did not understand grace and forgiveness. Since my mom didn't protect me and do what she said she was going to do, when I saw that in my wife, I became angrier and acted out above and beyond out of frustration. Through forgiveness, I now understand what salvation really means in physical terms. I knew God forgave me, but I really didn't know what forgiveness looked like. God used me needing to forgive my wife to save me and accept his forgiveness of my sins. Consequently, God used forgiving my wife to paint a picture of what Jesus' grace is to save me, and it made me immediately extend mercy to my wife and offer her forgiveness." Carlos continued to say, "Charles Townsend III influenced me the most in my marriage." He explained, "My response to the gospel required an action because my mind was renewed, therefore I had to demonstrate and walk that faith out in my day-to-day responses."

You can no longer allow anger, frustration, or pride to dictate your actions. The Purposeful Husband does not allow anger to drive his emotions. He acknowledges the hurt and acts with humility and grace when dealing with his wife. He calls on the name of Jesus and asks for strength and wisdom to handle situations that arise in his life. He surrounds himself with wise Godly counsel to lean on for strength. He does not allow worldly understanding to guide him through difficult situations and trials in life. He focuses on God's grace and how God dealt with our disobedience and unwillingness to do what is right. The Purposeful Husband quickly forgives and forgets all trespasses and does not hold his wife hostage after she hurts him. He finishes the race by continuing to show agape love to his wife no matter what occurs. Even when you feel like throwing in the towel, packing up all your belongings and running for the hills to get away from your cantankerous, evil, contrary, manipulating, lack of understanding creature you married and now fully regret marrying. The Purposeful Husband understands that his horizontal relationship with his wife is a mirror reflection of his vertical relationship with God. If the Purposeful Husband is experiencing hell with his wife, it is because he is doing the same thing with God. Dr. Tony Evans says, "You are not working to get grace, you are working because you have grace."

Points of Reflection

1. A Purposeful Husband focuses on being the husband God has called you to be. Ephesians 5:25-33

2. He forgives all trespasses. Luke 6:37

3. He shows grace and mercy with his actions and not just his words. 1 Timothy 1:16, Romans 9:15-16

Notes and Reflection

CHAPTER THIRTEEN

Finishing Strong

"The ultimate measure of a man is not where he stands in moments of comfort and convenience, but where he stands at times of challenge and controversy.
-Dr. Martin Luther King

CHAPTER 13

Finishing Strong

As Purposeful Husbands, we must remain focused on loving our wives and washing them in God's word regardless of how they treat and talk to us. The bible says in Ephesians 5:25-27, "Husbands, love your wives, just as Christ also loved the church and gave Himself up for her, so that he might sanctify her, having cleansed her by the washing of water with the word, that He might present to Himself the church in all her glory, having no spot or wrinkle or any such thing; but that she would be holy and blameless." Through prayer, fasting and consistently reading the word of God, we must understand that God is always in control. No matter what you may be physically going through and experiencing in your marriage, no situation is greater than God. We

Nobody wins in a divorce, in fact, everybody loses, especially your children.

often react to what is being said to us rather than focusing on listening to what God is calling us to do in our marriage.

There may come a time when your spouse decides it is over and leaves the house. When this happens do not be surprised, it is part of the plan. Satan's plan to destroy your marriage does not always come through someone outside your immediate family. It is highly likely to be through direct conflict with your wife. It could occur from your mother-in-law, or father-in-law. In fact, it could happen from your children or parents causing conflict in your marriage. Regardless of where it is stemming from, both spouses must be committed to God and each other and work through the conflict together. If either of you throws in the towel or quits, Satan has accomplished what he set out to do. Nobody wins in a divorce, in fact, everybody loses, especially your children. They may grow up dealing with abandonment issues, anger and frustration, low self-esteem, and several other issues. Children many times blame themselves after a divorce and believe they are the reason their parents are no longer together. Both parents and children should seek counseling to heal and recover from the divorce. Do not think for one second that everyone will walk away untouched from this situation. There will be wounds inflicted on everyone involved, and counseling should be sought to completely heal and move forward.

Consequently, if you find that you are walking down this path of divorce and separation from your wife and children, surround yourself with Godly friends. Do not attempt to walk alone during this season in your life. Realize and know that leaning on your own understanding at this point will cause you more harm than good. While you are under attack you need an army of saints praying with you and for you, encouraging you and your spouse as you transition during this season.

Points of Reflection

1. A Purposeful Husband realizes conflict in marriage should be handled with love and understanding. Ephesians 5:22-23

2. He recognizes just because his wife says it is over; it is not over until God has spoken. 1 Corinthians 7:12-15

3. He understands he needs to put on the whole armor of God because Satan seeks to destroy Christian marriages. Ephesians 6:10-20

Notes and Reflection

CHAPTER FOURTEEN

Faithfulness Over Foolishness

"God does his best work when things are dead."
-Pastor Lawrence Scott

CHAPTER 14

Faithfulness over Foolishness

In 2015, a close friend of mine found himself in a situation. After repeated attempts to save his marriage, including several rounds of marriage counseling, his wife moved in with her mother and refused to come home. You see, she had emotionally checked out of the marriage months prior but never said a word. So, after constant verbal arguments trying to get a response out of her husband failed, she decided to go another route. She accused him of trying to run her over with his vehicle to justify her desiring a separation. She told anybody who would listen, including several of their church members. When two concerned members called the husband and asked to hear his side of what occurred, the husband told them this was not true. No matter what he said, they refused to believe him because the lie had already taken root.

The real issue in the marriage was the mother-in-law had continually planted negative seeds about the husband, and his wife chose to believe her. In a final attempt to save their marriage, they both agreed to meet with their pastor. On the following Tuesday, when they were to meet, the husband arrived first. When he attempted to open the door to the church for his wife, he realized she had brought her mother with her. There was no way his mother-in-law would allow his wife to come alone and possibly reconcile. As I previously stated we must be careful who we are listening to.

During the meeting with their pastor, it became obvious that the marriage was over because only one person wanted to be married. The other chose her mother over her husband under the guise she was terrified of him, given he was a "maniac." We have to understand when people cannot control you, they try to control how others view you. So, they make up things about you to justify their actions. The reason I can recite this event so well is because this happened to me. This is my story, and I refused to listen to outside influences, well-meaning friends and family who told me, "Man just walk away, she chose her mother over you; run and don't look back." The flesh is weak,

> *"God is in control, turn your situation over to him."*

and under normal circumstances that is what would have happened. But my trust is in God, and he did not tell me to leave. The bible tells us in 2 Timothy 3 that difficult times will come. Verse 3 says, "We will be unloving, irreconcilable, malicious gossips, without self-control, brutal, haters of good." Although I did not know what was going on with my wife, I refused to walk away without consulting God. Consequently, this goes back to what I previously mentioned about being surrounded with Godly men who can encourage you and pray with you during rough times. Things may be going great one day and turn for the worse a day later. Because I was surrounded with mentors whom I trusted and respected, I reached out to them for counsel, rather than leaning on my own understanding. They all told me the same thing, "God is in control, turn your situation over to him." Even though the pain of abandonment and being hurt was overwhelming, I focused on God and not my situation. I asked Graddie should I step down from serving in the Audio Ministry with everything going on and the accusations being made. I explained how she was smearing my name around church, and I believed I needed to defend my character. In love, despite my lack of understanding, he told me, "No, keep your mouth closed, keep serving and let God handle it." Consequently, on the Sundays I was scheduled to serve on the sound board, I would start my morning off by playing Beverly Thomas song, "If The Lord Doesn't Do Anything Else For Me, He's Done Enough;" because in my soul I knew no matter how bad I felt or how hurt and heartbroken I was about what I was going through, I could recount how faithful God had been. I thought about the drunk driver who hit me in 2012 and left me for dead on Interstate 10, and how I walked away without a scratch even though I was not wearing a seatbelt because it was defective. I thought about my childhood when I was 8 years old and suffered from Bell 's palsy causing one side of my face to be paralyzed. And how my uncle Gilbert Bigham came over and prayed over me, asking God to make me whole and that I never suffer from that again. And God answered, and I have not had it since. So, I went down the list of every time God showed up in my life, and time after time, I could see his hedge of protection on my life. Even though the pain of abandonment and being hurt was overwhelming, coupled with the fact I was not allowed to have any contact with my son because he was not biologically mine, I focused on God and not my situation.

Even though the chapter is about me, I want you to understand this book is about God and his will for our lives. I shared my story to show you that God is in control. I did not understand at the time why I was going through the things I was experiencing while writing this book, but God had a master plan and it included having me experience the things he wanted me to include in this manuscript. The last four chapters were written while in the midst of a storm. I was forced to focus, study, and pray. In fact, I prayed more than I ever had in my life to stay on task in writing this book while facing all kinds of storms, threats, and personal attacks. Although the truth was revealed months later by one of her family members, I had already forgiven her and her mother earlier in the year. You see, God had me writing a chapter called, "Forgiveness On Steroids," while being angry at both for what was being done and said about me. I had to forgive them to move forward. The enemy tried everything known to man to stop me from writing and completing "The Purposeful Husband," because he knew someone would read these words and strive to be better. The Bible tells us, "Faith without works is dead." If you do not remember anything else in this book, remember to always choose faithfulness over foolishness. You will have trials in life, and it is all about how you respond as they occur.

Points for Reflection

1. A Purposeful Husband knows when people cannot control you, they try to control how others view you. Genesis 39:1-23

2. He puts his trust and focus on God, not his situation. Psalm 56:3, Proverbs 3:5-6

3. He knows it does not matter how bad things look, praise God for working it out. Psalms 34:1

Notes and Reflection

CHAPTER FIFTEEN

In Closing

"If you are going to be a better husband, you better be one now because the clock is ticking."
-ROYCE F. ROBINSON

CHAPTER 15

In Closing

By Alexander Williams

Men work and want to come home to a peaceful environment. The stressors of the world, that we do not openly discuss because we are manly men, are supposed to stay outside of our domicile. However, sometimes when you are married that is simply not a reality. One of the most uncomfortable things you may have to face in your life is going into battle with your wife. Your wife, the same lady you pledged to respect, honor and protect, is now one of your life's stressors. It is easy to just go through a daily routine of going to work and burying yourself in another activity, such as playing with the children until you both are tired, trying to avoid confrontation with your

God gave us spiritual armor for a reason, and the reason is not to sit on the sidelines of life.

spouse, but that does not help. Just because you ignore a wound, does not guarantee that it will heal over time. Unless you apply the proper treatment, and I must emphasize PROPER treatment, then you will lose in the end. Even worse, if you get into a routine of avoiding your spouse, you will open the door for others to come into that space in your soul.

God gave us spiritual armor for a reason, and the reason is not to sit on the sidelines of life. Armor is for battling as well as to protect you during a battle. If you remember that you are supposed to love your wife like Christ loved the church, you can win when experiencing conflict in your marriage. Jesus did not yell from another room while teaching the apostles and others. Nor did he beat people into submission when they did not heed his doctrine. Jesus sometimes had to pray past the point of exhaustion of all those around him, in the process of fulfilling his purpose and life's mission.

What is your purpose and mission with your wife? Are your goals, thoughts, and actions for your wife grounded in proper spiritual motivation? Are your requests made for the betterment of your marriage and family, or are your requests rooted in selfish desires? These are just the basic questions you need to ask yourself BEFORE heading towards your wife. Keep in mind, you are supposed to be a protector; if you are afraid to address issues with your spouse, eventually, she may start to question your manhood. Be bold and be loving when speaking to her. Do not speak with timid tones and fervor, but make sure you are not speaking to dominate her, because either extreme stance will not lead to success. Be prepared to explain your "whys" of the way you are thinking and what the ending results will be going down this path. Also, be prepared to be humble in being wrong, as well as being right about those uncomfortable situations. Eventually, your spouse will be willing to submit to your leadership if she recognizes you are basing your actions on God's word rather than your own thoughts and actions. If she decides not to submit to you as the head of the house, that is not your concern, pray about it and turn it over to God. Both spouses at times struggle with giving up individuality to become one after marriage. This may be one of the most difficult things you encounter after saying I do, but this may be one of the most rewarding encounters you may have. Becoming a Purposeful Husband will shape and mold your union for better or worse, so you need to make sure that you go into this battle with love in your heart and God in your soul.

Has this book helped you identify things you need to correct in yourself? If it has, I urge you to confess it and repent from it, so that God can wash you and your marriage whiter than snow.

Declaration

I _____ will become a Purposeful Husband. I will love, cherish, and encourage my wife daily. I will reject passivity and accept responsibility for my family. I will study God's word consistently and have my wife read and study God's word with me. I will pray with my wife and pray for my wife daily. I will remove all malice and negativity from my mind and heart. I will honor her and always lift her up, never ceasing to dwell on God's vision for my family. I will create a family mission statement and focus on living with Purpose. I will sew agape love into my marriage, my church, and my community, from this day forward.

X:_____ Date: _____

Study Questions

1. What can you do to become a Purposeful Husband?

2. What can you change about yourself to better understand God's plan for your life?

3. Write out your mission statement for your family.

4. List five things you noticed about your wife recently.

5. How has God's grace and mercy affected how you respond to your wife during an argument or disagreement?

6. Explain what forgiveness looks like to you in your marriage? Primarily in how you respond to your wife and children.

7. Define sacrifice and how you apply it in your marriage.

8. If you could start all over again from day 1 in your marriage, what would you do differently?

9. Have you experienced the power of forgiveness? Explain the benefits of letting go of grudges and hate.

10. List ways you can monitor your wife's love tank.

11. Describe the last time you planned a surprise date for your wife.

12. What is your wife's love language? And how have you been able to show her you recognized her love language?

13. How have you made a point to spend quality time with your wife? Kids?

14. Do you pray with your wife? How often?

15. Do you pray for your wife? How often?

16. On a scale of 1-10 with 10 being the highest, how would your wife rank you as a husband? Why?

17. What secrets have you been keeping from your wife? Why?

18. Do you have a Godly man, mentor or someone holding you accountable in your spiritual walk with Christ?

19. Who can you get to become your spiritual accountability partner?

20. Do you know someone who could benefit from reading The Purposeful Husband?

Afterword

This book was written out of love and obedience to God. I can honestly say I struggled with the decision to write this book when it was placed on my heart to write. I told God "Seriously, you want me to write a book on *Becoming The Husband God has called me to Be, and the Husband My Wife Needs me to Be*, are you sure?" I told God not only am I not qualified to write a book on this subject, but I am also not equipped to effectively communicate how to be something I am not myself. God spoke to me that day and said, "I didn't ask you to be equipped, qualified, or anything else. I want you to write what I tell you to put on paper. I will equip you and provide the knowledge you need to complete the task. Trust and believe in me that I will speak through you and use you to produce what I have called you to do.

I did not know I would go through a divorce while writing The Purposeful Husband. I struggled to continue during the storm I was experiencing at the time. I leaned on Graddie Peoples, Jeff Bailey, Joseph Adams Sr, and Paul Harris. I contemplated stepping down from serving in the Audio Ministry and shared this with them separately. And all of them had the same response, encouraging me to continue praying for my family, serving and allow God to fight my battle. I reluctantly obeyed and continued to focus on God and not my situation. Hurt and confused, I told myself I would never allow anyone to get close enough to hurt me again. Little did I know I would meet a phenomenal woman five years later named Terrell Lewis who would change my previous statement. As I am writing this, we are celebrating our first anniversary. By no means am I insinuating I have it all figured out, not even a little bit. However, I will put in the work to become the husband God has called me to be. With God's help and a consistent effort to learn his word, we can become Purposeful Husbands.

We want to hear from you, email the author at:
www.eew@eewilkins.com

Bibliography

1. Chandler, Matt. The Mingling of Souls Study Guide. David C. Cook, 2015.

2. Covey, Stephen R., et al. The 7 Habits of Highly Effective Marriages. Brilliance Audio, 2012. Audio CD.

3. Evans, Tony. Marriage: It's a Covenant, Not a Contract. 2017, Oak Cliff Bible Fellowship, Dallas, TX. The Urban Alternative.

4. Freesia, Theme. "8 Encouraging Quotes from Billy and Ruth Graham." Christ-Centered Mama, 2018, www.christandmama. com.

5. Goodreads. "Dwight L. Moody Quotes." Goodreads, 2018, www.goodreads.com.

6. King, Martin Luther, Jr. Strength to Love. Harper & Row, 1963.

7. Lewis, C. S. Letters of C. S. Lewis. Letter dated 8 Nov. 1952.

8. Loritts, Crawford. "Your Life, Your Legacy." Manifest Conference, Houston, TX, 2018. Conference Presentation.

9. Patrick, Darrin. The Dude's Guide to Manhood. Thomas Nelson, 2014.

10. Quintana, Armando. "22 Dave Ramsey Quotes Which Will Help You Learn How to Manage Your Money and Be Debt Free." Addicted 2 Success, www.addicted2success.com.

11. Robinson, Royce F. "Managing Marital Conflict." Crossover Bible Fellowship, 22 August 2015. Sermon

12. Scott, Laurence. "The Church That's Lit." Crossover Bible Fellowship, Mar. 2020. Sermon.

13. Thomas, Gary L. Thirsting for God. Harvest House Publishers, 2011.

14. Tripp, Paul David. What Did You Expect? Redeeming the Realities of Marriage. Redesign ed., Crossway, 2015.

15. Wilson, Blake. "When God Shows Up." Sermon, 2018.

16. Ziglar, Zig. Great Quotes from Zig Ziglar: 250 Inspirational Quotes from the Master Motivator and Friends. Gramercy, 1997.

17. "Purposeful." Merriam-Webster.com Dictionary, Merriam-Webster, www.merriam-webster.com/dictionary/purposeful. Accessed 21 Apr. 2021.

18. Cover photo by Pearl via Lightstock.com

Scriptures

1. Genesis 1:7, 2:24

2. Deuteronomy 24:5

3. Joshua 1:8

4. Psalms 1, 119:97-99

5. Proverbs 13:20, 15:18, 22, 16:3, 18, 18:21, 20:7, 22:6, 24:27, 27:17

6. Isaiah 54:17, 64:6

7. Jeremiah 17:9

8. Lamentations 3:22-23

9. Habakkuk 2:2-3

10. Matthew 6:14-15, 18:21-22, 19:8-9

11. John 14:27

12. Romans 12:1-2

13. 1 Corinthians 7:5, 11:3, 16:14

14. Ephesians 4:2, 9-12, 15, 27, 31-32, 5:25

15. Ephesians 5:33, 6:12, 6:10-17

16. Philippians 2:3-4, 4:8-9, 4:19

17. Colossians 3:2, 12-14, 19

18. 1 Timothy 3:4-5, 5:8

19. 2 Timothy 3:17

20. Hebrews 13:7

21. James 1:5-8, 19-20, 22-25, 26

22. 1 Peter 3:7, 4:8, 10

23. 1 John 4:18-19

Books to Read

1. Manhood Restored: How the Gospel Makes Men Whole by Dr. Eric Mason (2013)
   A biblical call for men to reclaim their identity and purpose through the power of the gospel.
   Buy on Amazon

2. The 5 Love Languages: The Secret to Love That Lasts by Gary Chapman (1992)
   Explores how understanding your spouse's primary love language can transform your relationship.
   Buy on Amazon

3. Kingdom Man: Every Man's Destiny, Every Woman's Dream by Dr. Tony Evans (2012)
   Challenges men to step up as spiritual leaders in their homes and communities, under God's authority.
   Buy on Amazon

4. The Dude's Guide to Manhood: Finding True Manliness in a World of Counterfeits by Darrin Patrick (2014)
   Offers practical wisdom on being a godly man in today's culture without falling into stereotypes.
   Buy on Amazon

5. What Did You Expect?: Redeeming the Realities of Marriage by Paul David Tripp (2010)
   Confronts common marriage struggles with biblical principles and gospel-centered solutions.
   Buy on Amazon

6. The Mingling of Souls: God's Design for Love, Marriage, Sex, and Redemption by Matt Chandler (2015)
   A candid look at love, attraction, and intimacy through the lens of the Song of Solomon.
   Buy on Amazon

7. Your Marriage Today...And Tomorrow by Dr. Crawford Loritts (2016)
   Encourages couples to build a marriage legacy that honors God and impacts future generations.
   Buy on Amazon

8. Sacred Marriage: What If God Designed Marriage to Make Us Holy More Than to Make Us Happy? by Gary Thomas (2000)
   Reframes marriage as a spiritual discipline intended to shape us into the image of Christ.
   Buy on Amazon

9. Marriage God's Way: A Biblical Recipe for Healthy, Joyful, Christ-Centered Relationships by Scott LaPierre (2016)
   A straightforward, Scripture-rich guide for couples seeking a biblical foundation for marriage.
   Buy on Amazon

10. When Sinners Say "I Do": Discovering the Power of the Gospel for Marriage by Dave Harvey (2007)
    Emphasizes grace and forgiveness as essential ingredients in every gospel-centered marriage.
    Buy on Amazon

Family photo taken by Shannon White

Eric Eugene (E.E.) Wilkins works for a fortune 500 company and has 25 years of Conflict Resolution Experience. The Houston based author's passion for Marriage and Family Life, led to him writing The Purposeful˚ Husband. He serves in the Membership & Maturity Ministry, at Crossover Bible Fellowship, in Houston, Texas with his wife Terrell; and has a 9-year-old daughter, named Amirikal, who loves stuffed teddy bears.

You can schedule E.E. Wilkins for a speaking engagement, or order additional copies of this book, by contacting him at www.eewilkins.com or email eew@eewilkins.com

We want to hear from you, contact us at:
www.eewilkins.com

www.ingramcontent.com/pod-product-compliance
Lightning Source LLC
Chambersburg PA
CBHW070337130626
46556CB00007B/2912